HANDS-ON SCIENCE

THINGS THAT GROW

Step-by-Step Science Activity Projects
from the Smithsonian Institution

Gareth Stevens Publishing
MILWAUKEE

For a free catalog describing Gareth Stevens' list of high-quality books, call 1-800-341-3569 (USA) or 1-800-461-9120 (Canada).

ISBN 0-8368-0959-9

Produced and published by

Gareth Stevens Publishing
1555 North RiverCenter Drive, Suite 201
Milwaukee, Wisconsin 53212, USA

Series editor: Patricia Lantier-Sampon
Book Designer: Sabine Beaupré
Editorial assistants: Jamie Daniel and Diane Laska

Printed in the United States of America

1 2 3 4 5 6 7 8 9 98 97 96 95 94 93

CONTENTS

Weights and Measures Abbreviation Key

U.S. Units

in = inch	oz = ounce
ft = foot	qt = quart
tsp = teaspoon	gal = gallon
T = tablespoon	lb = pound
C = cup	°F = °Fahrenheit

Metric Units

cm = centimeter	kg = kilogram
m = meter	km = kilometer
ml = milliliter	°C = °Centigrade
l = liter	
g = gram	

INTRODUCTION

By the 21st century, our society will demand that all its citizens possess basic competencies in the fundamentals of science and technology. As science becomes the dominant subject of the workplace, it is important to equip children with an understanding and appreciation of science early in their lives.

Learning can, and does, occur in many places and many situations. Learning occurs in school, at home, and on the trip between home and school. This book provides suggestions for interactive science activities that can be done in a variety of settings, using inexpensive and readily available materials. The experiments, activities, crafts, and games included in this book allow you, whether teacher or parent, to learn science along with the children.

SOME SUGGESTIONS FOR TEACHERS

The activities in this book should be used as supplements to your normal classroom science curricula. Since they were originally developed for use in out-of-school situations, they may require some minor modifications to permit a larger number of children to participate. Nonetheless, you will find that these activities lend themselves to a fun-filled science lesson for all participants.

SOME SUGGESTIONS FOR PARENTS

One of the most important jobs you have as a parent is the education of your children. Every day is filled with opportunities for you to actively participate in your child's learning. Through the **Hands-On Science** projects, you can explore the natural world together and make connections between classroom lessons and real-life situations.

FOR BOTH TEACHERS AND PARENTS

The best things you can bring to each activity are your experience, your interest, and, most importantly, your enthusiasm. These materials were designed to be both educational and enjoyable. They offer opportunities for discovery, creative thinking, and fun.

HOW TO USE THIS BOOK

There are ten activities in this book. Since every classroom and family is different, not all activities will be equally suitable. Browse through the book and find the ones that seem to make sense for your class or family. There is no prescribed order to these activities, nor any necessity to do all of them.

At the beginning of each activity is a list of all the materials you will need to do the project. Try to assemble all of these items before you begin. The procedures have been laid out in an easy-to-follow, step-by-step guide. If you follow these directions, you should have no difficulty doing the activity. Once you have completed the basic activity, there are also suggested variations that you can try, now or later. At the end of each activity is an "Afterwords" section to provide additional information.

SUN TRAP

SUN TRAP

1/2 in = 1.27 cm	150,300 gal = 568,735 l
2 in = 5.1 cm	162,000 gal = 613,000 l
14 in x 12 in x 10 in =	11,700 gal = 44,272 l
35.5 cm x 30.5 cm x 25.4	

A Sun Trap takes from 60 to 90 minutes to build. It also takes a sunny spot to succeed. A bright yard, fire escape, or window sill will do.

YOU WILL NEED

1 Cardboard box
  about 14" x 12" x 10"
8 Empty soup-size cans
4 Clear plastic bags
  or plastic wrap
2 Toothpicks
Sharp knife or scissors,
  masking tape, newspaper,
  ruler, pencil, water,
  aluminum foil
Room thermometer,
  rubber bands (optional)

At last you can do something about the weather. You can make it warmer, cooler, wetter, or drier in your own solar greenhouse or sun trap.

A solar greenhouse collects the sun's heat during the day and stores it until the heat is needed at night. Because it can store heat, a sun trap doesn't need much extra fuel to keep warm.

You can build your own solar greenhouse with these plans. In your own sun trap you can grow tropical plants, heat water, and dry fresh fruit.

CUTTING COMMENTS

It takes a lot of cutting to make a sun trap. You can use a scissors, but the best cutting tool is a sharp knife. When cutting with a knife, always try to:
■ cut away from yourself
■ place your fingers behind the blade
■ keep the knife in a safe spot. Never use a sharp knife without the permission or supervision of a responsible person.

1 If the cardboard box is not square, choose one of the longer sides to be the front. Label the sides with a pencil.
■ Cut the top off the box.
■ On the left front side, draw a line from the top left corner to the bottom right corner. Cut along this line.
■ On the right side, draw a line from the top right corner to the bottom left corner. Cut along this line.
■ Cut along the bottom front edge. Remove the cut pieces from the box.

2 Cut the bottom edge of the left side to the back. Cut the bottom edge of the right side to the

back. Tilt the back wall of the box forward about two inches. This will direct more sunlight to the center of your greenhouse where your plants will be.

3 Carefully, turn the box over. Mark the excess cardboard on the right side. Cut off the excess. Mark the excess cardboard on the left side. Cut off the excess.

4 Tape the bottom edges together on both sides with masking tape. Be sure the edges are airtight. Cut off the extra cardboard across the bottom.

5 Cut vents in the middle of the bottom of the left and right sides. Open the vents so that the flaps are on the outside. Vents will help cool your greenhouse in the summer and give plants the fresh air they need.

6 Tape several layers of newspaper to the outside of the back wall for insulation. Insulation will help keep your greenhouse warm in winter and cool in summer.

7 Cover the inside of the back wall with aluminum foil. This reflector will help aim sunlight toward the center of your greenhouse where the plants will be. It will also help warm the heat storage cans.

8 Tape together several clear plastic bags or pieces of plastic wrap to cover the front of the box. Tape one side to the bottom of the box. This plastic will let sunlight in and help keep heat in your sun trap. It will also help keep cold air and wind out, just like the glass in a greenhouse.

9 Fill the cans with water. Cover the top of each can with plastic held down with tape or a rubber band. These heat storage cans will collect and store heat from sunlight during the day. They will slowly give off that heat to warm the greenhouse at night.

10 Take your box, cans and tape outside to a sunny, dry, level spot. Even the edge of a front step will do. Face your greenhouse toward the sun.
■ Line with water-filled cans along the back wall of your sun trap.
■ Place the thermometer, if you have one, on the floor of the greenhouse to check temperature changes.

■ Tape the plastic over the front. Stretch it as tightly and smoothly as you can. This will let the most light through.
■ Close the vents and be sure your greenhouse is airtight.

If your greenhouse gets hotter than you want it to, prop the side vents open with toothpicks and unfold the top of the plastic cover one inch. Please note that your sun trap is not waterproof. Do not leave it outside in the rain or snow.

You can use your solar greenhouse for more than growing plants outside. Use it for starting seedlings, growing an herb garden, experimenting with heat, helping bread dough rise, and even drying fruit.

MAKE YOUR OWN RAISINS

You can turn your sun trap into a fruit dryer and make your own dried fruit. First, empty your sun trap.

■ Cut out the left and right sides leaving a one-half inch border. Cover the two side openings with cheesecloth.

■ Use cake cooling racks or other screen racks to make shelves inside. Lay whole seedless grapes or apple slices on the shelves.

■ Close the front plastic flap. Leave your sun trap in the sun all day, but bring it inside at night. In a few days, the fruit will be dried and ready to eat. Store fruit in an airtight jar until needed.

VARIATIONS

■ Set a can on a large piece of paper in the sun. Trace the can's shadow every hour. Decide which way your sun trap should face to catch the most sunshine.

■ Find four empty cans of equal size. Place an empty can, one filled with water, one with soil and one with rocks in the sun. Cover each with plastic and a rubber band. When they are warm, bring them indoors. Which stays warm the longest?

AFTERWORDS

As early as the first century A.D., Romans were growing fruit and vegetables in simple greenhouses. Large tubs were covered with clear sheets and heated with decomposing manure. A more elaborate greenhouse built at the same time was covered with rough glass and fitted with a hot air system. It was unearthed at Pompeii.

In Victorian England, greenhouses or conservatories were added to the homes of the wealthy. They were large enough to hold fruit trees. Parties were held in these rooms so guests could pick their own dessert. Later, some families had up to a dozen greenhouses: one for melons, one for strawberries, one for exotic giant water lilies, and so on.

Today, greenhouses are still used for growing tropical plants in non-tropical climates. They are also used for germinating seeds, extending the growing season, and other agricultural needs. Agriculturists grow many types of produce in greenhouses that they are unable to grow outdoors. Agriculturists have also been able to grow larger quantities of produce. It is possible to grow thirty times more lettuce per acre in a greenhouse than outside in a field. Fruits and vegetables grown in a greenhouse need much less water than those grown outdoors. Outside, one ton of tomatoes needs about 162,000 gallons of water. The same amount grown in a greenhouse would need only 11,700 gallons. That's a savings of 150,300 gallons of water! This savings alone would be reason enough to put all farming under glass — except for one thing. Many greenhouses have little insulation and heat storage.

To grow one ton of tomatoes, you would need as much as 100 times more oil to heat a greenhouse than would be needed outdoors.

In the 1930s and 1940s, greenhouse builders in New England sank their buildings partially in the ground to save fuel. They knew the surrounding earth would insulate the greenhouses.

Other fuel-saving methods were found. Gardeners learned that brick walls, rock beds, and barrels of water all act as "heat sinks," storing heat to keep a greenhouse warm after a sunny day. This was the beginning of "solar" greenhouses.

Solar greenhouses have been designed to collect and store energy in many ways. With rising heating and food costs, solar greenhouses have been put into use as simple home extensions. Many homeowners have turned the south-facing wall of their homes into efficient and attractive sun traps.

CRYSTAL GARDEN

CRYSTAL GARDEN

1/2 C = .12 l
1 C = .24 l
2 1/2 C = .6 l
5 in = 12.7 cm

Grow a colorful and crazy garden of crystals — in a bowl of rocks! It will take 20 minutes to set up your garden, and one or two days for the crystals to grow. While they're growing, you can do two more experiments to discover the secret nature of crystals.

YOU WILL NEED

1 Cup Epsom salts
½ Cup water
Food coloring
2 Small, shallow bowls
    about 5" in diameter
A few small rocks
Saucepan, spoon, stove
Magnifying glass (optional)

If you were on a scavenger hunt and had to find a crystal, what would you bring back? Rubies? Diamonds? A chandelier? Actually, there are plenty of crystals right in your own kitchen — for example, in your salt shaker and sugar bowl.

Salt and sugar crystals are so small, you might not have noticed how beautiful they are. By doing these easy experiments, you can watch some ordinary ingredients grow into jewels!

1 Place a few small stones in each of the two shallow bowls. In a saucepan, heat ½ cup water. Slowly add 1 cup of Epsom salts, stirring constantly. Make sure the salts dissolve completely, but do not let the mixture boil. Add a few drops of your favorite food coloring and stir again.

2 Now you can experiment with this mixture to find out how temperature affects the growth of crystals. Pour half of the mixture over the rocks in one bowl, and pour the other half into the second bowl. Set one dish in a warm place — over a heater or radiator, for instance. Put the other dish in a cool, but not cold, location. *After this, don't touch the bowls.*

3 Look at your Crystal Garden 6 hours later. Have the crystals started to form yet? Soon you will see a thin crust forming across the top of the mixture. Let the Crystal Garden sit *undisturbed* overnight.

4 The next day, gently break the crust on the bowl that was placed in a cool spot. Pour off any remaining liquid. What kind of crystals do you see? Are they large or small? Square or needle-like? You may want to use a magnifying glass to observe the crystals more closely. Wait another day, and then repeat this step with the bowl that was placed near the heater. How are these crystals different from the ones that were allowed to cool and form more quickly?

VARIATIONS

■ Find out whether crystals will grow in a bowl of marbles or nails. Will the crystals grow if you don't put anything else in the bowl with the Epsom salts mixture?
■ Try growing crystals from alum or sodium bicarbonate. Both should be available at your pharmacy.

ROCK CANDY RECIPE

You can grow big rock candy crystals and eat them, if you're willing to wait a week or more.

Caution: This activity needs close adult supervision. Remember: Sugar syrup gets very hot. Handle it carefully!

■ First, suspend a weighted string inside a glass, as shown in the illustration. You can use a steel nail, a button, or several paper clips as weights, but don't use anything made of lead.
■ Next, stir 2½ cups of sugar into 1 cup of water in a saucepan. Don't be surprised if all the sugar doesn't dissolve until after you heat it up — that's the idea. Heating the water

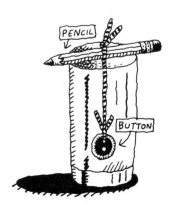

FAKE GLASS

causes the water molecules to move farther apart, and this makes room for more sugar. This is called a supersaturated solution. (In fact, the Epsom salts solution you made was a supersaturated one, too.) Heated, the water holds more sugar than it does when it's cold.

■ Cook the sugar syrup until it boils. Continue cooking over medium heat *without stirring* for three or four minutes.

■ Remove the syrup from the heat and let it cool for a minute or two. Then pour the syrup into the glass with the weighted string. Be careful, because if the syrup is too hot, the glass might break. Using a towel or potholder, place the glass somewhere where you and your family can see it easily. Let it stand *undisturbed* for a week or more, until the crystals have formed around the string. Be patient and *do not move the glass*.

If the whole glass of syrup crystalizes into one solid lump, you probably cooked the syrup too long or stirred it while it was boiling. Try again!

You'll enjoy watching the crystals every day, as they grow from tiny, perfect "starter" crystals to larger, more irregular chunks. How does the sugar crystal shape compare with the Epsom salts crystals you grew last week?

■ When the crystals are large enough, break your rock candy

into pieces and enjoy it — a little at a time! Let's face it — a lot of sugar just isn't good for your teeth.

LIGHTS! CAMERA! FAKE IT!

Did you ever wonder why stuntmen never flinch when they jump through a window or get hit over the head with a bottle? The answer is fake glass — and since it's made with plain old sugar, it's one of Hollywood's cheapest tricks.

To make fake glass, grease a cookie sheet and put it in the refrigerator to chill. Put ½ cup of sugar in a saucepan and heat it over a *very low flame* until the sugar melts and turns golden brown. (Sorry — homemade fake glass isn't clear.) **Be very careful and do not touch the syrup.** Sugar gets very hot! When the sugar melts, pour it onto the cold cookie sheet, tilting it to spread the syrup thin. Let cool. This is sugar glass — just like they use in Hollywood! It might be fun to smash your sugar glass into the kitchen sink and pretend you're in a smash hit Hollywood movie!

What's the difference between sugar glass and the rock candy you made? Why didn't the sugar glass form into crystals? If you think about your experiment with Epsom salts, can you guess the answer?

AFTERWORDS

Isn't it strange that the chandeliers and goblets we ordinarily call "crystal" are actually only glass? True crystals are very unlike glass, both in the way they are formed and the way they look. By definition, a crystal is any substance in which the atoms come together in a regular, organized pattern. The atoms in salt, for example, will always arrange themselves in exactly the same way, forming a six-sided box. The atoms in sugar form a different pattern, creating a rectangular crystal that is slanted at both ends. Each and every kind of crystal, from a ruby to a grain of sand, has its own unique arrangement of atoms that result in a variety of crystal shapes. There are short, fat crystals and long, spikey crystals. Others are flat and sheet-like, or small but intricate like a snowflake. However, one thing holds true for all crystal types: They all have flat sides, which are called faces. And regardless of the crystal's shape, the angle between each set of faces is always the same.

For crystals to form, the atoms in the crystal substance must be able to move around freely, so that they can arrange themselves in their particular pattern. This is possible only when the crystal substance is dissolved in solution, or heated to a liquid, or "molten," state. As you saw when you grew Epsom salt crystals, the time it takes for the solution to cool affects the size of the resulting crystals. When a solution is cooled quickly, the atoms arrange themselves into many smaller crystals. When a solution is cooled slowly, the atoms arrange themselves into larger crystals. Once a solution has completely cooled, the atoms are no longer free to move around and the crystal-forming process stops. When the earth's crust cooled millions of years ago, this same principle applied. The crystalline materials near the surface cooled more quickly than the matter deeper underground. Consequently, the crystals that formed near the surface were rather small, and the ones underground became large rocks.

But what happens when a crystal substance is melted and then cooled so quickly that the atoms don't have time to arrange themselves at all? What happens is shown by your sugar-glass experiment; in fact, that's also what happens when sand is made into glass. Glass is a very thick, super-cooled substance in which the atoms are disorganized — just like the atoms in a liquid are. Unlike the atoms in crystals, the atoms in liquids form no particular pattern and are constantly moving around. For this reason, strange as it may sound, glass is sometimes called a liquid by scientists because it has all the properties of a liquid. And even though the atoms in glass are moving around *very* slowly, they are still moving enough to allow the glass to *flow* like a liquid, over a period of time. If you've ever seen a 200-year-old house with its original windowpanes intact, like the ones at Colonial Williamsburg in Virginia, you can see that the glass is actually thicker at the bottom of the pane than at the top. Scientists think this is because the glass is very slowly flowing downward. But it would take an *eternity* for a windowpane to flow into a puddle of glass!

SPINY STUNTS

SPINY STUNTS

55° F = 13° C
60° F = 16°C

Spiny Stunts takes about 20 minutes to complete. It is most successful when done during the cactus' growing season—spring or summer.

YOU WILL NEED

2 Small, column-like cacti of about the same diameter
Clean, sharp knife or single-edged razor blade
Alcohol, shoelaces or yarn, cotton
Newspaper or paper towel

It's easy to make new plants grow from two old ones—just graft them together! Grafting is a simple way of growing two similar plants from the same set of roots. Plant growers use grafting to make new varieties of plants from old varieties.

You can make your own original cactus combinations by grafting a tall cactus top to a short cactus bottom, a bald top to a hairy bottom, or a flat top to a round bottom—or try your own Spiny Stunts!

BEFORE YOU START:
When is a Cactus Not a Cactus?

To do successful Spiny Stunts, both plants that you use must be members of the cactus family. Cacti have spines, but not every spiny plant is a cactus. Some members of the Euphorbia (you-for-bee-uh) and milkweed families that live in the desert are also spiny and can look very much like cacti.

To tell the difference between a real cactus and an impostor, look at the plant's spines. Cacti have cushiony bud-like areas on their stems from which spines, flowers, and hair grow. Spines grow *only* from these buds. In milkweed and Euphorbia plants, spines grow directly from the stem instead of from buds.

A second way to identify a cactus impostor is to stick it with a pin. If a milky-white liquid oozes from the plant, it is not a cactus, but a Euphorbia. Be careful—the milky Euphorbia liquid can irritate your skin and eyes. (If you accidentally come in contact with it, wash the area thoroughly with soap and water.)

KEEPING THINGS CLEAN

Cactus grafting is an operation that you can do on plants. Just as in any operation, it is important to keep everything as clean as you can. Otherwise, germs will get into the cacti's wounds and the cacti won't heal properly.

1 Dip your knife in alcohol to sterilize it. Let it air dry. Be careful not to touch the blade of the knife again before grafting your cacti. Wrap a paper towel or a piece of newspaper around

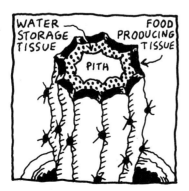

each cactus to protect your fingers from the cactus spines. Find a section of each cactus that is about the same thickness. Cut off the top of each cactus with a horizontal cut at that spot. Remember not to touch the open wounds — it's important to keep the cut surfaces germ-free.

2 Look closely at the insides of the two cacti. You will be able to see three layers of tissue. The outer green tissue produces food for the plant. The lighter green tissue in the second layer stores water. The white, inner "pith" contains the growth rings of the cactus. These growth rings make the cactus grow outward from its center.

3 Switch the tops of the two cacti. Put the top of one cactus on the base of the other, and vice versa. Line up the piths of the two cacti as closely as you can. The piths must eventually grow together for the cacti to keep living.

4 With a cotton ball to protect your fingers, push the top cacti firmly onto the bottom cacti. This will remove any air bubbles

between the two. Use a cotton ball to pad the top of the cacti. Tie the cacti in place with shoelaces or yarn.

5 Place your new plants in a sunny window. Keep the cacti warm and the grafts dry and clean. After 3 to 4 weeks, remove the yarn from your cacti and gently wiggle their tops to make sure that the grafts have healed completely. (If the grafts have not healed, make new cuts and start again.) Then enjoy your original houseplant!

CACTUS CARE

Cacti grow at different rates during the winter and summer. For this reason, your cactus will require special kinds of care during different times of the year. A cactus' growing period occurs in the spring and summer. During these months, place your cacti in full sunlight—outdoors if possible. Water your cacti whenever the soil is dry. A small cactus may need water every few days, while a larger cactus will need water less often. When in doubt, wait another day before watering. It's better to under-water your cacti than to over-water them.

During the winter, a cactus enters a rest, or dormant, period. It is important that your cacti have an undisturbed dormant period to get ready for the next growing season. Place your cacti in a cooler location; 55 to 60°F is a good temperature for the winter. Keep your cacti dry; they will be able to store enough water to go 3 to 4 weeks between waterings. Soon after the dormant period, your cacti may begin to flower. Look for buds in February or March.

AFTERWORDS

Grafting cacti can be a sticky business—a real spiny stunt. But the cactus family is exceptionally tolerant of the grafting process. Almost all kinds of cacti can be grafted as long as they are healthy, the cuts are kept clean, and the piths line up closely.

Cactus grafts are successful because all cacti have an active cambium layer inside their piths. The cambium layer is thin tissue that produces new cells that control the cactus' sideward, or lateral, growth. These new cells pass food and water up and down

the entire plant. Because it is possible to connect the cambium layer of one cactus to another, cactus grafts "take" readily and the rootstock of a healthy plant can pass food to its more fragile grafted top.

Cactus grafting is fun and produces an unlimited number of "living sculptures." However, horticulturists (people who grow fruits, vegetables, flowers, and plants) also graft cacti for practical reasons.

Occasionally, a cactus grower will find a plant that is unlike any of the thousands produced from the same parent plants. A genetic change makes the difference. These cacti are rare and often beautiful. Unfortunately, they are also often weak and cannot live long on their own. To make sure the most beautiful or unusual part of the cactus survives, a cactus grower grafts it to a normal cactus with a hardy set of roots, or rootstock.

A striking example of using grafting to save an unusual plant is in the case of albinos. Albino cacti lack the green chlorophyll they need to produce their own food. These "sports" can be bright red, pink, or yellow, instead of

green. Without chlorophyll, the albino cacti will die. Cactus growers provide these cacti with a constant food source by grafting the albinos on to healthy green rootstocks.

Cacti aren't the only plants that are grafted. Many fruits are grown from grafted plants. Apple trees are grafted to produce better varieties of apples. Sometimes apple growers graft branches from tall apple trees onto short apple trees. Then they can reach the fruit without using ladders.

Every time you eat a seedless orange, you are eating fruit from a grafted plant. Seedless oranges have no seeds to plant to grow new trees. Orange growers grow more "seedless orange trees" by grafting the fruit-making branches onto the roots of other orange trees.

You can't graft every kind of plant together, but you can make some funny combinations. Sometimes fruit growers can grow a couple of different fruits on the same tree. For example, they can graft a branch from an apricot tree onto a plum tree. The result is plum strange: a tree that grows both apricots *and* plums.

A SHOOT
IN THE DARK

A SHOOT IN THE DARK

A Shoot in the Dark takes only a few minutes to start. It will take about one week to finish the whole experiment.

YOU WILL NEED

1 Bowl or saucer of water
2 Flowerpots or
    other containers
12 Bean or pea seeds
    (lima, navy, etc.)
Potting soil

It's no accident that plants growing in the sunlight are green. The green color comes from chlorophyll. Together, sunlight and chlorophyll help plants produce their own food in a process called photosynthesis. What happens when a tender, young shoot finds itself trapped in the dark? Try this simple experiment and find out.

1 Place the 12 bean or pea seeds in a bowl or saucer. Soak the seeds in water for a day, until the seed coats wrinkle and crack.

2 Fill the two flowerpots or other containers with soil, leaving about one inch of space at the top of the pot. Place six seeds, evenly spaced, on the surface of the soil. Cover the seeds with about one-half inch of potting soil. Water thoroughly.

3 Place one pot in an undisturbed dark place, such as the back of an unused closet or drawer. It is important to keep this pot in *complete* darkness. Even a few seconds of light can change the results of the experiment.
■ Place the second pot in a sunny window.

4 Let the plants grow for 5 to 10 days. During this time, water the seeds in each pot equally—once every day or two.
■ Remember, you must keep the dark seedlings in total darkness, so be sure the room is completely dark when you open the closet or drawer to water them.

5 When the plants in the sun are about six inches tall and have several leaves, bring the second pot out of the darkness. Place the plants side by side.

6 Compare the plants grown in light with the plants grown in darkness.
■ Are they the same size? If not, which plants are taller?
■ Is there any difference in color?
■ How many leaves does each plant have?
■ How do their roots compare? To find out, carefully dig one plant in each pot out of the soil.

VARIATIONS

■ Put both pots from the experiment into the sunshine. How do the plants grown in the dark change when you put them in a light place?
■ How much light do plants need for normal growth? Grow a few seeds in the dark. Bring them out into the light for 10 minutes a day. How do these plants compare with plants grown completely in the dark or in the light?
■ Try this experiment you can eat. Put several dozen mung beans or alfalfa seeds in a clean jar. Rinse the seeds well, pour off any extra water, and put the jar in a dark place. Rinse the seeds thoroughly twice a day and keep them in the dark until your sprouts are ready. Enjoy them in salads, sandwiches, and Chinese dishes.

AFTERWORDS

It's hard to believe that a big plant can grow from just a tiny seed. It's especially amazing when you see how little of the seed is the new plant. For example, look inside a peanut (or an acorn, or lima bean, or pumpkin or sunflower seed). If you split the peanut in two, you will see the little peanut plant inside. The rest of the peanut is food the plant uses until it's big enough to make its own food through photosynthesis.

When you plant a seed in the ground, it starts to grow very quickly. First, it sends down roots to hold it in place in the soil. Then it sends up a hook-shaped shoot that pushes through the soil easily. A seedling's survival depends entirely upon its ability to find light. Without light to provide the energy for photosynthesis, a plant quickly dies. While the plant is still underground, it has no light. It uses the food inside the seed to grow. As the plant gets bigger, it uses more and more of the food inside the seed. By the time you can see the plant stem coming up through the soil, there isn't much food left in the seed at all.

After the stem comes up through the soil, leaves appear. At an earlier stage, leaves might make it hard for the plant to break through the soil into the sunlight. Once the plant is in sunlight, the green leaves help the plant make its own food through photosynthesis.

FOOD

PEANUT PLANT

In A Shoot in the Dark, the dark closet or drawer acts like the underground conditions of a planted bean. The plants you grew in the dark have the same features as normally grown plants before they push through the soil surface. Their shoot tips are hooked and their shoots are white, elongated, and leafless. Once dark-grown seedlings are moved into the sunlight, leaves and green color quickly develop. Plants need only a short flash of light to begin the developmental processes necessary for photosynthesis.

Botanists (people who study plants) often grow seedlings under dark conditions to study plant growth. Dark-grown seedlings, also called "etoliated seedlings," are also used in the study of plant colorings other than green chlorophyll. More common uses of etoliated seedlings include growing bean sprouts for cooking. Raising etoliated sprouts eliminates the green chlorophyll that gives some plants a bitter taste.

Your findings from this experiment can be applied to your own houseplants. Houseplants often do not receive enough light in homes. Plants that live in poor light become pale, weak, and will not flower. To keep your houseplants healthy, you must provide them with enough sun, or artificial light, or a combination of both. They then will be able to produce enough of their own food to grow and flower. While some plants can grow in the shade, no plant can remain a shoot in the dark for long.

1/2 in = 1.27 cm
1 in = 2.54 cm
6 in = 15.2 cm

FANCY PLANTS

FANCY PLANTS

1/2 in = 1.27 cm
1 in = 2.54 cm

It'll take only 90 minutes to set up this activity, but you'll have to wait a week or two before your Fancy Plants take on the color of spring.

YOU WILL NEED

Scissors, pen
1 Sponge
A small plate
Grass seed or ryegrass
    seed, radish seeds,
    and mung beans
Plastic wrap, plastic bags
1 Styrofoam cup
Cotton balls
Paper towels
Empty egg carton, yogurt
    container, or similar boxes
Soil
Old shirt with pocket
Jar with a screw top
Black construction paper

Why do you think plants grow in the ground? And why *don't* they grow on park benches, or on tabletops, or on the roofs of parked cars? If your answer is "Plants need soil to grow in," you'll be surprised to find out that just isn't true! At least, it isn't *always* true. You can grow some plants — like grass, for instance — in sponges, on paper towels, and maybe even in a shirt! Use your imagination and come up with as many different Fancy Plants as you can.

1 Use a scissors to cut a sponge into a 1″ wide snake shape. Soak the snake sponge in water, and put it on a small shallow plate. Carefully plant the sponge with grass seed, making sure you push some of the seeds into the holes in the sponge. Cover the plate with plastic wrap. Set the plate near a window. Keep the sponge wet, and watch for roots. Remove the plastic wrap when green appears. Water the snake-in-the-grass several times a day!

2 Now, let's see if this experiment works with other things. Draw a face on the outside of a Styrofoam cup. Fill the cup with cotton balls soaked in water. Sprinkle grass seed on top of the cotton balls and seal the whole cup in a plastic bag. When the green grass "hair" grows, remove the plastic bag and water the grass frequently.

3 Fill the sections of an empty egg carton with various soil substitutes, such as sand, crumpled tissues, tiny pebbles, sawdust, clean cat litter, loose tea, marbles, or whatever else you can think of. Fill one section of the egg carton with soil. This will be the "control" part of this experiment. Plant some radish seeds in each section of the egg carton. Water every day. What do you notice about the roots? Do the radishes grow better when you put the egg carton in a closet for the first few days? Which part of the plant grows better in the dark — the leaves or the roots?

4 Try planting some grass seed in the pocket of an old shirt. Hang the shirt on a hanger and water or mist it frequently. Seal it in a plastic bag until the grass sprouts.

5 Watch seeds grow by planting mung beans in a screw-top jar lined with a sheet of black construction paper. The seeds should go between the black paper and the jar. Fill the center of the jar with wet paper towels, and add 1/2″ of water to the jar to keep the whole thing moist. Screw the lid on and lay the jar on its side. You'll be able to see roots and shoots growing against the black-paper liner within a week.

STAY IN CONTROL

With any science experiment, it's important that you, the scientist, remain in control. *You* must control the conditions of the experiment and *you* control the "variables" — the things that could change and affect the results of the experiment. That's why it's a good idea to have what scientists call the "control group" in your experiment. For instance, in Fancy Plants, you will plant grass seed in a sponge. But what if it doesn't grow? Is it

because the sponge isn't a good place for the seeds, or because there isn't enough warmth and light? Is there too much water, or not enough, in the sponge? The only way to find out for sure is to plant some of the same kind of grass seed in soil and take care of it in exactly the same way and at the same time as you do your experiment. This will be your control group. Set the control group in the same location with the seeded sponge. Water them both at the same time, with the same amount of water. Now you are in control of the experiment. If the grass planted in soil grows better than the grass planted in the sponge, you'll know that the sponge was the only reason for the difference in the results!

AFTERWORDS

As easy as it is to start grass or radishes in such unlikely places as a sponge or a shirt, these plants won't live long without constant attention and nurturing. You probably wouldn't want to spend the time it would take to keep your grass snake growing forever. But sometimes it *is* worthwhile to invest the extra time and technology needed to grow plants without soil. This method is called hydroponics. By looking at the techniques used in hydroponics, you'll discover why *soil* is such a perfect place for plants.

Water, air, light, warmth, nutrients, and stability. In just about that order, those are the things plants need to grow and thrive. With water at the top of the list, it's not surprising that some of the first experiments with soil substitutes involved using plain water as the growing medium. In fact, the word hydroponics comes from the Greek word for water. But, as early researchers soon found, there are a number of problems with trying to grow plants in a big tub of water.

The first problem is that water does not support a root system. To give plants stability, they must be suspended above the water tank by some sort of structure or base. Another problem is that water doesn't allow oxygen to flow freely to the roots. To cope with that deficiency, some hydroponic systems add air to the water with a motorized piece of equipment, a lot like the one you might use on a tropical fish tank. But then there's the question of nutrients. Elements like nitrogen, potassium, phosphorus, magnesium, and calcium are needed in relatively large amounts, and trace elements like iron, copper, and zinc are needed in tiny amounts. Water doesn't have a rich supply of these elements, and no matter how long the plants grow, the water won't be able to produce the nutrients or renew them over a period of time. They must be purchased and added in carefully controlled amounts, over and over again.

These drawbacks led many hydroponic growers to switch from just water to water and gravel as a growing medium, because gravel makes a sturdy base for the roots. But since gravel doesn't contain *any* nutrients and doesn't retain water, this method presents a whole new set of problems that must be overcome.

Now how does all of this compare with the time-honored method of growing plants in soil? Not too well. Without any supervision from the grower, *good* soil gives plants stability for their root systems. It also allows plenty of oxygen to reach the roots, and it contains most of the nutrients needed for growth. And unlike sand, gravel, loose tea, cat litter, sponges, and whatever else you might have experimented with in Fancy Plants, good soil can *hold onto* the water it receives for more than an hour. Generally speaking, good soil just naturally provides the things plants need.

But admittedly, not all soil is good soil. And in some parts of the world the time and expense needed to make the land ready for planting is overwhelming. In those regions, hydroponics is a "natural" choice — a way to supply locally grown crops at a lower cost.

MUD PIES

MUD PIES

Ummmm, delicious! A nice big plate of mud! Take about 30 minutes to dig the hole and plant the seeds. Wait 1 to 1½ weeks for them to sprout and find out who likes mud pies better — plants or kids!

YOU WILL NEED

4 Aluminum pie pans (disposable)
Shovel to dig soil, or large bag of potting soil
Pencil
Paper
Transparent tape
Nail
Popcorn kernels
Water
Large plate
A brick or piece of sandstone
Paper bag
Hammer
Dried-up modeling clay
Dried leaves, roots, and twigs
Food scraps such as carrot peelings, bread crumbs, and eggshells
Sand

What could be mushier, squishier, and gushier than a nice big mud pie! But plants are usually found in rich soil — not mud. What's the difference between mud and soil? Make your own mud pies and find out. And while you're waiting for your garden pies to sprout, you can also find out how long it takes nature to "make" soil out of the things that go into it.

1 If you can get permission to dig in your yard or somewhere in your neighborhood — great! Go outside and dig a hole about 18″ deep. Take enough soil from the hole to completely fill 3 aluminum pie pans. Make sure the soil doesn't have plants already growing in it. (If you are digging in a grassy area, throw the grassy part away, and use the dirt below the grass roots.) Put soil from near the top of the hole — the topsoil — into two of the pie pans. Put soil from the bottom of the hole — the subsoil — into the third pie pan. Label the first two pies "Topsoil" and the

third pie "Subsoil."

If you can't find a place to dig, use potting soil from a garden shop for this activity. Fill *only one* pie pan with potting soil and label it "Soil without drainage holes." Then go on to Step 2.

2 Use a nail to punch about 20 to 30 holes in the bottom of an empty aluminum pie pan. Fill this pie pan with topsoil transferred from one of the other two pans, or use potting soil. For this pie, make a new label that says "Soil with drainage holes."

3 Sprinkle 1 or 2 tablespoons of unpopped popcorn kernels on each mud pie. Mix the popcorn into the dirt, so that the kernels are underneath the soil. Now water each of the three pies thoroughly, but first put the pie with drainage holes on a large plate to catch the water that drips out. Set all three mud pies in a sunny place. Water them often enough to keep the mud pies muddy — but do not *overwater* the one with drainage holes.

Which pie is the first one to sprout? Does the popcorn grow better in the subsoil mud pie, in the topsoil mud pie, or in the topsoil pie with drainage holes? What do you think plants in the pie with drainage holes get that they don't get in the mud pie that is constantly soaked with water?

4 While you're waiting for your mud pies to turn into popcorn pies, try making some soil of your own! First you will need to "weather," or break down, some rocks. Since you don't have a million years and an ocean full of water to do this, you'll have to use a hammer instead. Take a brick or large piece of sandstone outdoors and put it in a paper bag on the ground. Through the bag, hammer the brick or stone until it crumbles into tiny pieces. Put the crushed rock into an empty pie pan.

Do the same thing with a dried-up piece of clay. Hammer it until it is powdery and add it to the crushed rocks. Add some dried leaves and grass, dead bugs, roots, vegetable scraps, a little bit of sand, and then water the whole thing. Use just enough water to keep the contents moist, but not soupy. Stir up the pie. Now let your pie stand for — how long? A week? A month? How long will it take to make soil? Mix the pie up every few days, and sprinkle with water if it dries out completely. Even if it never really looks like soil, try planting popcorn in it to see what happens.

AFTERWORDS

The story of soil is a long one, starting back to when the Earth's crust was first cooling. There was no soil or dirt then — just rock. But over a period of thousands of years, little bits and pieces of rock were broken off. Some rocks were worn down by the rain and wind. Others were dissolved by acids in the water of lakes and oceans. And many huge boulders were cracked again and again — into smaller and smaller pieces — by the changes in temperature from freezing winter to scorching summer.

But crushed rocks aren't the only ingredient in soil. You also need water, oxygen, and *organic material*, which is what we call things that either *are* alive or *were* alive. So here comes the big question: Where did organic material, like plants for instance, come from if there wasn't any soil to grow them in?

Scientists think that life began in the oceans and crept slowly toward land. It took eons for the tiny bacteria and protozoa of the water to evolve into forms of life that could survive on land. Step by step, inch by inch, larger life-forms developed. When they died, they became the raw material to form soil, which in turn became a good place for even larger plants to grow.

Dead plants and animals are important ingredients of the soil, but *live* plants and animals play a primary role, too. Take worms, for instance. Without worms, many of the dead leaves from plants and crops would just lie there on top of the field, or be blown away. But earthworms take little bits of dried leaves with them down into the earth as they tunnel around. One scientist found that the worms in a 3-foot-square area could take as much as 20 pounds of dead leaves underground in just six months time!

In moist soils, earthworms are numerous. In some parts of the world, there are 2 million earthworms per acre! An average acre, though, would only have about 50,000 worms in it, all working to mix up the soil. Their burrowing also brings minerals from the layers of subsoil *up* to the topsoil. And their movement opens up air passages and keeps the soil loose so that water can enter the ground and plant roots can grow more easily. Other animals that live underground — such as moles, ants, and beetles — do the same job. But what turns the dead leaves and insects into soil?

Bacteria are microscopic plants that are present everywhere on Earth. If you thought there were a lot of earthworms in an acre, just think of this: As many as 50 *billion* bacteria are in one drop of water! A rule in science says that the smaller an organism is, the more of them you'll find — and the greater an effect they'll have on the environment. That law is definitely true when it comes to bacteria.

Bacteria perform two main jobs in helping to make soil and keeping the soil "healthy" so that plants can grow. First, bacteria cause dead plants and animals to *decompose*, or break down into simpler elements. Without bacteria, dead things wouldn't rot or decay. Second, a gas in the soil called *nitrogen* is essential for all living things. Some bacteria are called nitrogen "fixers," which means they help plants to use the nitrogen present in the soil.

So the next time you want to make mud pies, go right ahead. But do it with a little respect! After all: It took the earth a long time to produce that beautiful black stuff you call mud!

GARDEN IN A GLASS

GARDEN IN A GLASS

If you like plants and gardens, this project is for you! It is also a quick way to have a garden of your own, especially if you don't have room for one outdoors.

YOU WILL NEED

Some empty, wide-mouth glass jars with lids — the bigger the better (A pickle jar from a restaurant is great! Ask around.)

Baking soda

Some pebbles

From a gardener's shop: small quantities of horticultural charcoal, standard potting soil, vermiculite or perlite, peat moss, sharp sand (or aquarium sand), bone meal (if available), and some small plants (or find them in a vacant lot)

Pan or basin or pail for mixing soil

Old nylon stockings

Scraps of jagged rocks or pretty stones

Pieces of wood that are worn from being outdoors

Scissors, spoon

Some Plasticine or modeling clay

1 Wash and rinse your pickle jar. Sprinkle 2 or 3 tablespoons of baking soda on the inside of the lid and add some water; this helps get rid of the vinegar smell. Lay your pickle jar on its side between two magazines or books so it can't roll.

2 Wash and rinse enough pebbles to make a ½" to 1" layer on the bottom of your jar. Take ⅓ as much charcoal and wash it: Put it in a pan or basin, add water, stir, and carefully pour off the dirty water. (You might want to use a strainer.) Sprinkle charcoal evenly over the rocks. These rocks and charcoal are your garden's "drainage bed."

The charcoal acts as a filter and lets clean water run down onto the rocks.

3 Cut up some old nylons; overlap the pieces to make a thin layer to cover your drainage bed. This *separator* will keep soil from getting into the bed.

4 Mix up your soil, following this recipe: 6 cups standard potting soil, 2 cups vermiculite or perlite, 2 cups peat moss, 1 cup sharp sand or aquarium sand (if you use beach sand, be sure to wash it well — just like the charcoal), and 1 cup horticultural charcoal. If you can find bone meal, mix in ⅓ cup. If you can't get these things, try ordinary soil from your yard.

5 Now, let your imagination run wild and design your garden! You may want to make it look like a little piece of the real world with hills and pathways. Look for pretty stones or rocks and twigs. Think of a tiny plant as a tree; create a forest!

6 Use a spoon to landscape your garden. Sprinkle some of your soil over the separator. You will need enough soil to cover the roots of your tiny plants. Dig holes in the soil where you want your plants to go.

7 If your plant is potted, hold it upside down in one hand. Gently tap the rim of the pot on the edge of a table or sink. (Cover the floor underneath with newspaper, to catch any loose soil.) Slip the pot off the plant. Knock much of the dirt off the roots. Pop your plants into their holes. Switch them around until you like the way things look. Then, gently pat the soil around each plant. Take out any extra soil. Spoon a bit of water around each plant, a spoonful at a time. Don't soak the soil!

1/2 in = 1.27 cm	2 C = .48 l
1 in = 2.54 cm	3 C = .72 l
3 T = 45 ml	2 T = 30 ml
1/3 C = .08 l	6 C = 1.4 l
1 C = .24 l	

8 Screw the lid on tight and put your new *terrarium* near a bright window—but **not in direct sunlight!** (You can use plugs of Plasticine or modeling clay as wedges to keep it from rolling.) If a place is comfortable for *you* (not too hot, not too cold), it will likely be comfortable for your plants. Your plants will grow and lean toward the light, so turn your terrarium around once in a while.

9 Now, check your "sprinkler system." You should always be able to see some water droplets on the inside of the glass. If there are so many that you can't see inside the jar at all, there may be too much water in your terrarium's "atmosphere." In that case, take the lid off for a few hours. Or it may be that the sunlight is too strong; try a shadier place. If there are *no* water droplets, add some water to the soil.

Once you get a nice bit of moisture on the glass you can tighten the lid, leave it tight—and that's it! So just sit back and watch your garden grow! You'll probably never have to worry about watering your plants ever again.

VARIATIONS

■ You may want to try a terrarium with cactus plants. You will need sandy soil. Here's the formula: Mix together 1 cup potting soil, 3 cups sand, 1 cup perlite, 1 cup charcoal, and 1 cup peat moss. This garden will need very little water and very little drainage. (Cover the surface with sand to make it look like a desert.)

You can leave the lid off.

■ If you have mosses and ferns growing in your yard, you can make a sealed terrarium for these. Use the standard mix recipe but add extra peat moss. Or try planting a terrarium with whatever small plants you can find in a lawn or vacant lot.

■ Sometimes a pickle jar sitting upright with just one or two plants makes a neat terrarium. How can you decorate the lid? Make a cradle out of soft rope or cord (macrame) and hang up your garden.

LARGE PICKLE JAR FROM RESTAURANT

SMALL TWIG CAN LOOK LIKE TREE

ADD PART OF PLANT FROM POT

AFTER PLANTING YOUR GARDEN, SCREW THE LID ON TIGHT

TOY HOUSE

DRIFTWOOD PRETTY STONE

USE PLASTICINE TO SECURE JAR

COLORED MARBLE

PAINTED EXTERIOR TO HIDE MATERIALS

PIECE OF GLASS LOOKS LIKE POND

PLASTICINE

■ What other containers can you use for terrariums? Glasses, bowls, jars, an old aquarium are possibilities; use plastic wrap to cover them. The bottoms from the biggest plastic pop bottles are great! Just cut the bottle's top off; remove the green or black plastic bottom and plant your garden in it. Then turn the bottle bottom upside down and use it as the terrarium cover. You could make these for gifts!

AFTERWORDS

Dr. Nathaniel Ward, an English surgeon, living in the 1820s, was interested in moths. He put the cocoon of a sphinx moth in some damp soil in a glass jar and put the lid on. He looked at it often, hoping to see the adult moth getting out of its cocoon. But he also noticed that some grass and a small fern had sprouted from the soil. Being a scientist, he was of course interested in the unexpected and decided to see how long the green plants would live in the sealed jar. They were still doing fine four years later, but then the jar was damaged while he was away. (No one remembers what happened to the moth!)

How do the water drop-lets get up on the inside of the jar? You put the water into the soil. When plants are growing, their roots absorb water from the soil. This water goes up through the stem to the leaves. Inside the leaves, the plant uses some of the water to make food for itself, to grow. But there is more water in the leaves than the plant needs and this extra water is given off by the leaves. This process is called *transpiration*.

Water that has been trans-pired goes into the air in the jar in the form of a gas, or *vapor*. When this water vapor reaches the cool, inner surface of the jar, it condenses to form tiny drops of liquid water. These tiny drops run together to form the tiny droplets you can see. Gradually, these drop-lets will run down the wall and into the drainage area. From here the roots pick up the water again and the whole business repeats itself. The trip that the water takes from the soil, through the plant and the leaves, into the air, onto the wall and back into the soil is called a *water cycle*.

How can your plant breathe if the jar is sealed?

Plants take in *oxygen* and give out *carbon dioxide* — just like you do! Green plants also *photosynthesize* in sunlight. In photosynthesis, plants *take in* carbon dioxide and *give off* oxygen (and some water). So the plant recycles its own carbon dioxide and oxygen. Tiny organisms in the soil cause dead *organic* (once alive) particles also in the soil to *decompose*, or decay, gradu-ally. As they decompose, the particles release carbon diox-ide into the air in the jar.

Plants also need the element *nitrogen* to make proteins. But these protein molecules lock up nitrogen inside the growing plant. You may see your plants grow for a while and then stop. Some of the leaves may wilt, dry up, and fall off into the soil. Don't worry! Soil organisms will decay the dead leaves and release their nitrogen. This nitrogen goes back into your plants and they will perk up again. This completes the *nitrogen cycle*.

These cycles will repeat over and over again, re-creat-ing an "atmosphere" just like the Earth's. Your terrarium really is a miniature world!

SLIME TIME

SLIME TIME

2 in = 5.1 cm   11 in = 27.9 cm
3 in = 7.6 cm   14 in = 35.6 cm
4 in = 10.2 cm

Jeepers creepers—it's slime time! Time to get down in the dirt and find out what it's like to live in the world of earthworms. It will take about an hour to build a home for worms—and then you really ought to keep an eye on them all month.

YOU WILL NEED

Small, heavy cardboard carton
Utility knife or scissors
Acrylic "box"-style picture frame about 11" by 14", or sheet of acrylic 11" by 14"
Ruler
Pencil
Masking tape or stapler
Plastic garbage bag
Duct tape
Trowel or small shovel
Potting soil
Aluminum foil
Old bath towel

1 To make a Worm World for earthworms, you will need to construct a vertical box that is open at the top and covered on one side with acrylic. Begin by cutting your carton down to size: Cut the top part off so that you are left with a box that is 4" deep. If the bottom of the box happens to be exactly the same size as your picture frame, great! Go on to Step 3. If not, you will need to cut the box down some more.

2 Measure your acrylic sheet or plastic box-style picture frame. (Be sure to use the inside dimensions of the frame.) Now draw dotted lines on the bottom of the box to match the dimensions of the picture frame, measuring from 1 corner of the box. Cut along the dotted lines, as shown in the illustration. You will have three pieces of the box when you are done. Part A is the main part of the Worm World. Part B will form the other side of the Worm World box. Part C can be thrown away. By fitting A and B together and letting them overlap, you will have reconstructed a box, that will be 11" by 14" and open on one end. Tape or staple A and B together to make the box stronger. When you are done, you should have a box that is open on top and open at one end.

KEEP THE WORM WORLD OUTSIDE IN A GARAGE OR PATIO

COVER TOP WITH ALUMINUM FOIL

ST/88

3 Now you will need to make the box water-proof. Line the bottom and sides with a plastic garbage bag, and tape the bag in place using duct tape. Don't open the garbage bag up; use it as a double layer. Be sure the box is completely covered with plastic on all of its inside surfaces. Use plenty of tape to seal the plastic to the box.

4 Place the acrylic picture frame over the box, to make the window through which you can view the worms. The picture frame should fit snugly. One end of the box will still be partly open, but that's all right. That is the top opening for your Worm World. Use duct tape to tape the acrylic to the box on three sides. Seal it well. If you are using a sheet of acrylic instead of a picture frame, use a double layer of tape to make the box stronger.

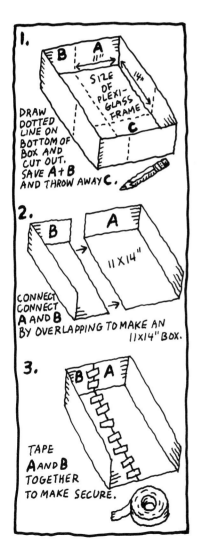

1. SIZE OF PLEXI-GLASS FRAME — B A 11" 14"
DRAW DOTTED LINE ON BOTTOM OF BOX AND CUT OUT. SAVE A + B AND THROW AWAY C.

2. B A 11 X 14"
CONNECT A AND B BY OVERLAPPING TO MAKE AN 11X14" BOX.

3. B A
TAPE A AND B TOGETHER TO MAKE SECURE.

LINE INSIDE OF BOX WITH GARBAGE BAGS AND TAPE IN PLACE. TOP IS OPEN DUCT TAPE

5 Stand the Worm World box on end, with the opening up. The box is now ready to be filled with layers of dirt. Each layer should be about 2" deep. Use alternate layers of topsoil, potting soil, and sand. Or dig some soil from two different areas—one where the soil is rich and black, another where the soil is light brown. Pack the soil down firmly as you fill the Worm World so that there are no big air spaces. To keep the earthworms from getting out, don't fill the Worm World to the top. Leave about 3 inches from the top layer of dirt to the top of the box. Water the soil so that it is quite moist but not soaking, and keep it wet by sprinkling it every few days.

6 Now it's Slime Time! Use a trowel or small shovel to dig for earthworms in your yard or in a park. (Be sure to get permission if you are digging in a public area.) Be careful not to cut the worms in half or injure them while you are digging. Handle them carefully. Place 2 or 3 good-size worms on top of the soil in your Worm World. Add a few rotting leaves on top, which the worms will eat. If you have room, you may want to keep the Worm World outside in a garage or patio. If you want to keep it indoors, cover the top with a piece of aluminum foil, punctured with small air holes. Cover the whole thing with an old towel to keep the Worm World dark.

When you are all done with the experiment at the end of the month, let the worms go—back to their real worm world!

HOW TO WATCH WORMS

■ Earthworms are night crawlers. They move around when it's dark. By putting a towel over the Worm World, you have created artificial darkness. When you take the cover off, the worms may crawl away from the light. To watch them for a long period of time, go outside at night and use a flashlight covered with a red balloon. The red light will not disturb the worms. You can go looking for earthworms this way in your yard or park at night too.

WHAT TO LOOK FOR

■ Look for the tunnels earthworms make through the layers of soil. How long will it take the worms to mix up the different layers of soil?

■ Try to see the worms as they eat. They will pull a rotting leaf partway into their tunnels and nibble on it. Sometimes they poke their heads up aboveground and eat leaves. Where are their tails?

■ Can you tell which end is the worm's head? Can you find its mouth? Are some worms fat and some skinny? Look closely: Does the same worm always stay the same shape?

AFTERWORDS

Next time you sit down to eat a BLT or a peanut butter and jelly sandwich, just remember this: You should thank your lucky worms for all the food you have to eat. Without earthworms, we would not have the kind of soil that we have on much of the earth. Without earthworms, very little food would grow. Earthworms are called "nature's plows" because as they tunnel through the earth, they mix up the soil layers, allowing air to get in and making space for plant roots to grow. They eat leaves and decaying animal fragments, which pass through them and then come out as *castings*. The castings fertilize the soil, providing food for plants. Without worms, the earth would be too hard, compacted, and lifeless to grow tomatoes or peanuts for your favorite lunch.

When you went digging for earthworms, could you tell in advance whether you would find worms just by looking at the topsoil? Was the soil a rich, black color, loose and crumbly? If so, you probably found lots of earthworms there. If the soil was hard and dry, on the other hand, with very little growing in it, you probably didn't find any. In some rich farmland areas, you could find 1 million worms on every acre of land! These earthworms can turn and churn 40 tons of topsoil per acre in a year.

Some people think that if you cut an earthworm in half, it will grow back, or *regenerate,* the missing parts. Actually, earthworms can regenerate their heads or their tails, but only if they are severed before the first 10 segments or after the last four. They can even regenerate their brains!

Did you notice a wide, lightcolored band around the body of the worms in your Worm World? That is called the saddle, or *clitellum.* Earthworms are hermaphrodites, which means that they are not male or female but *both.* All earthworms can produce eggs and can fertilize each other, but they cannot fertilize themselves. To mate, any two earthworms join together at the clitellum, fertilize each other's eggs, and then each one makes an egg case, which is deposited in the soil. If your earthworms did not have a clitellum, they were not adult worms. Maybe you had Teenage Slime Time instead!

You probably noticed that even without a cover on your Worm World, the earthworms do not try to escape. That's because they don't really want to be anywhere but inside the earth. Even when they're feeding, worms will often leave their tails anchored underground for self-protection. That way, if a robin tries to pull the earthworm out of its burrow, the worm can put up a fight. Usually, though, the robin will win the tug-of-war. Other burrowing animals such as moles will dig them out of the soil and eat them. Skunks and owls eat earthworms, too. If it weren't for these enemies, earthworms could live to be 10 years old.

Even though they have no ears or eyes, earthworms seem to have many senses. They respond to light by moving away from it, and they respond to vibrations, too. In some parts of the country, where earthworms are used as fishing bait, people use vibrations to drive worms out of the ground! They hammer a wooden stake into the ground and then beat on it. The vibrations are transferred through the soil and the worms sense danger.

ALIENS

ALIENS

Is there life in outer space? Will alien beings ever come to Earth? Scientists have several methods of finding out and here's one way. It will only take you 30 minutes to set up the experiment, but you may not see results for several weeks.

YOU WILL NEED

4 Empty jars with lids
Hot water
Measuring cup
Saucepan
Unflavored gelatin
Spoon
Pen or marker
Paper
Tape
Scissors
String

Extraterrestrials…alien life-forms…little green kids from outer space. Are they out there—and, if so, what do they look like? What if the aliens aren't *large* visible beings that walk and talk? What if they are too small to be easily seen?

That is the problem scientists had to deal with in the 1960s and '70s, when the Viking spacecraft was being designed to land on Mars. Scientists needed a way to detect *any* life-forms—even tiny, microscopic ones, like bacteria. One of the experiments designed for the Viking project was called Gulliver. In the Gulliver test, "sticky" string would be dragged across the surface of Mars. Then the string would be put in a container with "food," so that if any life-forms were stuck to the string, they would be nourished and grow.

You can try a version of the Gulliver experiment yourself here on Earth. Who knows? Maybe you'll find life-forms in places you never even *suspected* could sustain life—maybe in your closet or under your bed!

1 First, you will need to sterilize your jars, to remove any life-forms (germs, for instance) that are already there. To do this, wash the jars and then pour boiling water into them. The jars will be hot, so **don't touch them now.** Let them stand until they are cool. Sterilize the jar lids in the same way, by pouring boiling water on them. **Be very careful when using the stove to boil water.** You may want to have an adult help you with this.

2 Measure 2 cups of very hot tap water into a saucepan. Add one packet of unflavored gelatin and stir until the gelatin is completely dissolved. You may need to heat the water and gelatin over low heat to help the gelatin dissolve. Pour 1/4 cup of gelatin into one of the jars and screw the lid on tight. Label the jar "control." Then pour 1/4 cup of gelatin into each of the other three jars.

3 Cut 3 pieces of string, each about 15 inches long. Dip one of the pieces into the remaining gelatin in the pan and leave it there for a minute, until the string is soaked. Then take the string and drag it across the floor somewhere—under your bed, across the living-room rug, across the basement floor, or wherever you like. Put the string into one of the jars and screw the lid on. Label the jar with "Rug" or "Basement" or wherever the sample came from. Soak the other 2 pieces of string in gelatin and go outside to repeat the experiment. You might want to drag one of the strings across the grass or dirt and the other across the sidewalk. Label these samples, after putting each into a jar, and put the lids on both of them.

4 Now, wait and watch. Check your jars for life-forms every day. It might take two weeks or more before you see a change in the gelatin—or on the string. And remember: The life-forms you are looking for are tiny, like bacteria. They probably won't grow into big, ugly green blobs! But the important

thing is that you're discovering life-forms where you didn't think they existed!

Is there anything happening in the control jar? If so, that shows you that your jars had bacteria in them even before you put the string samples in.

VARIATIONS

■ Leave the sticky string outside for several hours before sealing it in the jar.
■ Punch holes in the lids of the jars so that any alien beings present will have an air supply.

■ Use a string soaked in apple juice and a string soaked in gelatin to collect life-forms outside. Leave them both in the sun for an hour or so. Does the apple juice attract a life-form different than the kind attracted to the gelatin?

WHAT IS A CONTROL?

Whenever you conduct a scientific experiment, you are asking a "what if" question. For instance, you might ask "What will happen if I pile 726 cement blocks on my bicycle?" The answer is that the bike would be crushed! If you actually tried this experiment, you wouldn't need a "control," because you would have no doubt that the results came from only one cause: the cement blocks!

But for some experiments, you can't be sure what is causing the results. For instance, this month you are asking "What will happen if I drag some string on the ground and then seal it in a jar with gelatin?" If something starts to grow in the jar, are you sure it came from the string? Or did some life-forms fall into the jar while you were dragging the string around? In these cases, you need to set up two sam-

ples. You do your experiment on one of the samples, and leave the other sample — the control — alone. If the results you were looking for occur only on the experimental sample and not on the control, then you know exactly what caused the results.

AFTERWORDS

Searching for life on Mars or any other planet is a lot more difficult than you might think. For one thing, scientists must make sure that they don't contaminate the planet they are visiting by bringing along life-forms from Earth. When the Viking mission was launched in 1975, both of the spacecrafts — Viking 1 and Viking 2 — had to be entirely sterilized to kill all bacteria or other microorganisms that might be present. Can you imagine pouring boiling water on a spaceship? Actually, the Vikings were heated to 235 °F, then sealed inside a shield to keep out microorganisms.

Landing on Mars wasn't easy. On Earth, parachutes are often used when we want to drop people or objects out of the sky and land them safely on the ground. But the atmosphere on Earth is very dense compared with the atmos-

phere on Mars. That means that when parachutes open above Earth, the atmosphere is "thick" enough to push against the parachute material and cause it to slow down. On Mars, the atmosphere is so thin that it doesn't create much resistance. To jump out of a plane above Mars, you'd need a very big parachute!

To solve this problem and help the Viking lander get from the orbiter to the surface of Mars, scientists decided to use a combination of parachute and rocket engines. The rockets would help the lander set itself down gently. Unfortunately, the rockets themselves posed a new problem, because they tended to blow the soil in every direction. Scientists wanted to be sure the lander didn't mess up the soil directly surrounding the landing area, because that was the soil that would be sampled for the biology tests. Eventually, a better design for the rocket engines was found.

Did scientists find evidence of life on Mars? The results were mixed. Biologists generally agree that life-forms can be detected three ways: (1) You could look for evidence that some kind of food had been produced; (2) you

could look for evidence that food had been consumed; and (3) you could look for changes in the atmospheric gases — which is another way of saying that someone, or something, is breathing. (On Earth, atmospheric gases change when plants give off oxygen or when people exhale carbon dioxide.)

Although scientists didn't find any signs of food being produced, they did discover, during several experiments, that atmospheric gases changed quite a bit. However, the changes were not necessarily the kind that would indicate the presence of life-forms. Other experiments showed results that could easily have been caused by the presence of microorganisms — or could have been caused by strange chemical reactions on the planet. And when the Martian soil was finally analyzed, no organic molecules were found.

So what's next? Another trip to Mars — or maybe to that great, gassy planet Jupiter? Someday, you may be on board when another sticky string is cast into the vast universe, in search of aliens.

SHOO FLY, FRUIT FLY

SHOO FLY, FRUIT FLY

Don't say "Shoo, fly!" to fruit flies. They may be pesty, but scientists love to study them and so will you. You can raise two whole generations of fruit flies in a month (but it's best to try it in a *summer* month). It will take you 15 minutes to set up a habitat for them, and 30 minutes to observe them up close.

YOU WILL NEED

3 Large empty glass jars
Very ripe grapes and
    bananas
Paper towels
Absorbent cotton (large
    pieces, not cotton balls)
Sheet of notebook paper
Transparent tape
Very small clear glass or
    plastic bottle, such as an
    aspirin bottle
Aluminum foil
Magnifying glass

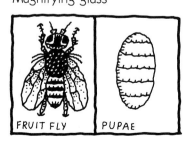

FRUIT FLY   PUPAE

Have you ever seen a bowl of fruit with fruit flies hovering around it? Did you wonder where the fruit flies came from? And why do they always seem to appear out of nowhere when fruit gets very ripe? It's easy to find out the answers by setting up a scientific experiment with two jars of fruit— one jar sealed up, the other jar open. Maybe the fruit flies are attracted to the ripe fruit. Or maybe the fruit-fly eggs are *on the fruit itself*—just waiting to hatch. Which is it?

1 Place half of a very ripe banana—with the peel still on—in a large, clean glass jar. Add some very ripe grapes and a crumpled paper towel. Close the mouth of the jar with loosely packed absorbent cotton, as shown. Make sure there are no holes around the edges, so that fruit flies can't get in or out.

1/2 in = 1.27 cm

2 Use a sheet of notebook paper and transparent tape to make a paper funnel that will fit in the mouth of the second jar. Let the small opening of the funnel be about ½" wide. Put some very ripe grapes and the other half of the banana in another jar, along with a crumpled paper towel. Set the paper funnel in the mouth of the jar. This forms a sort of trap, so that fruit flies can get *into* the jar but won't find their way *out* so easily.

3 Set both jars in a warm, bright spot, but not in direct sunlight. Within a few days, you should see some fruit flies. Are there fruit flies in both jars? Where did they come from? When you see 5 to 8 fruit flies in the jar with the funnel, remove the funnel and plug the mouth of the jar with absorbent cotton so they can't get out.

4 Watch the life cycle of the fruit flies in your jars. The eggs will be too tiny to see. But you can watch for the *larvae*—the crawling, worm-like stage in the development of the fruit fly. You might see them on the crumpled paper towel. They will eat the fruit for about a week and then change into the *pupae* stage. The pupae are almost adults, but not quite. When the pupae become adults, they will mate and then lay eggs. A few days after that, you will see new larvae, and the cycle will start all over again. Fruit flies live about four weeks all together. Count the fruit flies in your jar and see how fast they multiply.

5 Carefully transfer one or two of the new fruit flies to a very small empty jar, like an aspirin bottle. Wrap aluminum foil around the top two-thirds of the bottle, to make it dark inside. The fruit flies will move toward the light at the uncovered end of the bottle. Use a magnifying glass to observe them. Females are larger than the males. But

males have a larger, darker black band on the end on their abdomens. Can you tell which is which? If you think you have a male and female in your small bottle, transfer these fruit flies to the third large glass jar and add some fruit. Plug the opening with absorbent cotton. If you were right, these two fruit flies will mate and lay eggs. You can raise a whole new generation of fruit flies this way.

VARIATIONS

■ Place fruit in a jar but *do not* cover it at all. You may want to place the jar outdoors. Do fruit flies hover around the fruit? For how many days? Will they lay eggs and start a new generation? Does the fruit-fly population increase?
■ Try to raise fruit flies using different kinds of fruit. Find out whether or not you will get fruit flies with an apple, a pear, some cherries, or a peach.

AFTERWORDS

No matter how annoying it is to see a swarm of fruit flies circling around a beautiful bowl of fruit, scientists have often been willing to put up with the little buggers because fruit flies are perfect for one thing: the study of *genetics.* Genetics is the study of genes, and how different characteristics are passed along from parents to offspring. With fruit flies, which live for only about four weeks, a geneticist can follow 25 generations of fruit flies in a year! Fruit flies are also easy for scientists to obtain. Since fruit flies thrive in a warm environment— such as overripe fruit —scientists have a constant supply.

The fruit flies you raised are called *Drosophila*—the same species used in the study of genes. Imagine that you had a male fruit fly with curly wings and a female fruit fly with normal wings. Will their children have curly or normal wings? It only takes four weeks to find out, because the whole life cycle of the fruit fly is complete in that amount of time.

Drosophila have very large chromosomes— although all chromosomes are microscopic—which makes them easy to study. When the genes for several different traits are located together on one chromosome, scientists say that those genes are *linked.* So what happens if the gene for curly wings is linked to the male sex gene? In that case, only the male offspring of the fruit fly will have curly wings. Scientists have found that the fruit fly has more than 400 different genes, many of them linked together, so that there are a great number of variations in the ways fruit flies develop.

Can you see the color of your fruit flies' eyes? Believe it or not, they come in red, purple, white, apricot, and brown—not to mention the "bar-eyed" fruit flies and the ones with no eyes at all! Some of these colors are *dominant,* meaning that if only one parent passes that gene along to the child, the child will have the dominant trait. Other eye colors are *recessive* traits, meaning that *both* parents must pass the gene along in order for the child to have that trait. The same is true in human beings. Some eye colors are dominant— brown, for instance. Other eye colors, such as blue, are recessive.

Surprisingly, some genes for eye color in fruit flies are linked to the gene that determines life expectancy. How long will a purple-eyed fruit fly live? Only about 27 days. Fruit flies with normal eyes will live about 10 days longer.

Of course, fruit flies *are* pests, and they've done enormous amounts of damage as well. The Mediterranean fruit fly took hold in Florida in the 1920s, threatening to destroy acres upon acres of fruit. Eliminating the Mediterranean fruit fly cost $6 million and the effort lasted for several years—only to have the "Med fly" pop up in California again in the 1970s.

Another damaging species is the Mexican fruit fly, which attacks citrus fruits. Then there's the apple maggot, the cherry fruit fly, the melon fly, and others that attack walnuts, celery, asparagus, and olives. And it's very hard to get rid of them.

Luckily for you, it's pretty easy to get rid of *your* fruit flies. Just dump the project in the trash, seal it—and keep your fruit in the refrigerator from now on!

FOR MORE INFORMATION . . .

Places to Write and Visit

Here are some places you can write or visit for more information about things that grow. When you write, include your name, address, and age, and be specific about the information you would like to receive. Don't forget to enclose a stamped, self-addressed envelope for a reply.

The Institute of Ecosystem Studies
The New York Botanical Garden
Route 44A
Millbrook, New York 12545
(Mailing address: Box AB
Millbrook, NY 12545)

The Nature Conservancy
1815 N. Lynn Street
Arlington, VA 22209

The Carl G. Fenner Museum and Environmental
    Education Center
2020 E. Mt. Good Hope Road
Lansing, MI 48910

Audubon Park and Zoological Museum
6500 Magazine Street
Audubon Park
New Orleans, Louisiana 70118
(Mailing address: P.O. Box 4327
New Orleans, LA 70178)

Further Reading about Things That Grow

Here are more books you can read about things that grow. Check your local library or bookstore to see if they have the books or can order them for you.

Amazing World of Plants. Marcus (Troll Associates)
Carnivorous Plants. Overbeck (Lerner Publications)
Eyewitness Books: Plants. Burne (Alfred A. Knopf)
How Plants Grow. Wilson (Larousse)
Plants, Seeds and Flowers. Sabin (Troll Associates)
Seeds to Plants: Projects with Botany. Bates (Watts)
Tiger Lilies and Other Beastly Plants. Ring (Walker & Co.)
Wild Green Things in the City: A Book of Weeds. Dowden (Crowell)
The World's Weirdest Plants. Quinn (Price Stern)

Hands-On Facts about Things That Grow

Did you know . . .

- greenhouses were already being used to cultivate plants as early as the first century A.D.?

- animals aren't the only living things that hibernate during the winter? Some plants do, too. For example, both cactus plants and the bulbs of perennial plants such as tulips and lilies need a winter rest period to replenish their supply of nutrients for the next growth season. During this period, the plants' need for water and nutrients temporarily "shuts down."

- some life-saving medicines such as penicillin are made from mold cultures?

- a farmer who wants to grow one ton of tomatoes out-of-doors will need 162,000 gallons (613,000 l) of water, while the same amount of tomatoes can be grown in a greenhouse using only 11,700 gallons (44,273 l) of water?

- the amount of moisture in the air can have a marked effect on our perception of the air's temperature? Warm air that has a high moisture content will feel hotter than dry air that is the same temperature.

- plants can be successfully grown without their roots ever coming near soil? Horticulturists have developed a process for growing perfectly good plants, including fruit and vegetable plants, in combinations of water and gravel. This process is called *hydroponics*.

- an average acre of soil is home to approximately 50,000 earthworms?

- earthworms living in an area that is three feet (9 m) square will take as many as 20 pounds (9 kg) of dead leaves underground in a period of just six months?

- if an earthworm's head is severed at some point along the first ten segments of its body, it will grow a new head? Of course, it also grows itself a new brain in the process!

GLOSSARY

botanist: a scientist specializing in the study of plants.

bud: the part of a plant that is made up of undeveloped, overlapping leaves. A bud often contains a developing flower.

bulb: a rounded, underground part of a plant from which a new plant can grow. Onions and garlic are bulbs; tulips and many other flowers grow from bulbs.

chlorophyll: the green pigment found in plants that absorbs energy from sunlight during the process of photosynthesis.

dormant: a period, usually in the winter for plants, during which a plant's nutritional and growth system temporarily shuts down.

ecology: the study of how people, plants, and animals co-exist in their habitats.

erosion: the process by which soil or rock is depleted or worn down by weather conditions, water, and cultivation.

etoliated seedling: a seedling that is grown exclusively in the dark.

hermaphrodite: a plant or animal that is neither just male or female, but both at once.

horticulturist: someone who studies the care and cultivation of plants.

hydroponics: a process by which plants are grown without using soil, but rather water or some combination of water and gravel.

organic material: material made up of decomposed plants and animals that were once alive.

perennial: a plant that can live for two or more years.

photosynthesis: the process by which plants convert sunlight into nutrients. The process of photosynthesis begins when chlorophyll in the leaves is activated by the sunlight.

root: the part of a plant that absorbs water and minerals from the soil to benefit the entire plant. Roots are most often found beneath the soil.

seedling: a newly-sprouted plant, usually very fragile.

subsoil: soil that is located beneath the topsoil and that does not have a high organic material component.

topsoil: the soil that makes up the first four inches or so of soil, containing a higher proportion of organic matter than soil deeper down.

transpiration: the process by which a plant growing on land releases water vapor, usually through its leaves.

variable: a factor in a scientific experiment that could change and effect the results.

INDEX